I'm Going To READ!™

These levels are meant only as guides;
you and your child can best choose a book that's right.

Level 1: Kindergarten–Grade 1 . . . Ages 4–6

- word bank to highlight new words
- consistent placement of text to promote readability
- easy words and phrases
- simple sentences build to make simple stories
- art and design help new readers decode text

Level 2: Grade 1 . . . Ages 6–7

- word bank to highlight new words
- rhyming texts introduced
- more difficult words, but vocabulary is still limited
- longer sentences and longer stories
- designed for easy readability

Level 3: Grade 2 . . . Ages 7–8

- richer vocabulary of up to 200 different words
- varied sentence structure
- high-interest stories with longer plots
- designed to promote independent reading

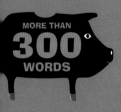

Level 4: Grades 3 and up . . . Ages 8 and up

- richer vocabulary of more than 300 different words
- short chapters, multiple stories, or poems
- more complex plots for the newly independent reader
- emphasis on reading for meaning

LEVEL 3

Library of Congress Cataloging-in-Publication Data Available

2 4 6 8 10 9 7 5 3 1

Published by Sterling Publishing Co., Inc.
387 Park Avenue South, New York, NY 10016
Text copyright © 2005 by Harriet Ziefert Inc.
Illustrations copyright © 2005 by Martha Gradisher
Distributed in Canada by Sterling Publishing
c/o Canadian Manda Group, 165 Dufferin Street
Toronto, Ontario, Canada M6K 3H6
Distributed in Great Britain and Europe by Chris Lloyd at Orca Book
Services, Stanley House, Fleets Lane, Poole BH15 3AJ, England
Distributed in Australia by Capricorn Link (Australia) Pty. Ltd.
P.O. Box 704, Windsor, NSW 2756, Australia

I'm Going To Read is a trademark of Sterling Publishing Co., Inc.

Sterling ISBN 1-4027-2108-0

A Class Play
with Ms. Vanilla

Pictures by Martha Gradisher

Sterling Publishing Co., Inc.
New York

Ms. Vanilla's class is happy today.
We are about to do a play.

The whole school
is sitting there.
"Open the curtain!"
says Mr. Blair.

"Our story begins
in a house by the wood.

It's the tale of
Little Red Riding Hood."

"Take this basket,
Little Red Riding Hood,
To Granny's house
through the big, dark wood."

"I'll sing as I walk
from tree to tree.
No wolf would dare
take a bite of me."

"Did you know that
trees can worry?

We wish Red Riding Hood
would hurry."

"We are the hunters
who sing a song,
And carry our guns
as we march along."

"I'm the wolf.
I'm mean, they say.
I want to eat everyone in the play.
I tied Granny behind the bed.
Now I'm waiting for Little Red."

"What big eyes you have!"
says Red Riding Hood.
"Granny, you don't look so good."

"What big teeth you have!"
says Red Riding Hood.
"Granny, you don't look so good."

"It's not your
Granny in the bed.
I'll eat you now!"
the mean wolf said.

"Look out, you wolf,
you're not so smart.
We've been watching you
from the start."

"We'll grab your tail.
We'll pull your paws.

We'll save Granny from your jaws."

"Now that Granny's
free at last,

We'd like to show you
our whole cast."

"Our play is over. We take a bow.
A big surprise is coming now!"

"Just to make our play a thriller,

The horrible wolf is . . ."

"Ms. Vanilla!"